REMEMBER ME...?

WHAT PART OF ME   VOLUME 1

*Thank You.
for spreading
the word.*

Toi Ragland

Toi Ragland (signature)

Bey Uni-Verse Enterprises LLC Minneapolis, MN

• • •

2nd Copyright ©2013 by Toi Ragland
3rd Copyright/ 2nd Editing ©2016 by Bey Uni-Verse Enterprises LLC

ISBN-13: 978-1480121034
ISBN-10: 1480121037

Book design, editing, and composition by Toi Ragland

Printed in the United States of America Republic Northwest Amexem, Alkebulan

* * *

Dedicated to those who are on a journey to finding their way, their cause and purpose in life. May you be open to growth, audacious to change and embrace each situation as it is presented to help define the better you...the new and improved you.

In Loving Memory of...

Constance Marie Hickman

Revonda (Danni) Mann

Karen Yolanda Smith

• • •

Acknowledgements

To my wonderful, intelligent, and loving husband Troy Bey, thank you for your daily words of encouragement, heaving out such remarkable potential in me, being a great teacher and loving me in my moments. To my children, Destinee and Princeton, thank you for allowing mommy to set an awesome example for yourselves in life, as a wife, mother and woman, you are truly my motivation. My mom, who has diligently told me "You are GREAT in everything that you do" and who believe in my talents. Thank you, mom, for always being proud of me. My dad, thank you for explaining characteristics about me that I didn't understand and challenging me to never give up. And to a host of family and friends, thank you for being so supportive of my words and encouraging me to shine through my God given talents.

Special Thanks

Shatuan Collins, Erica (cousin/sister) Harris-Jones, Evelyn Williams and April Brigham

Love You Always & Forever

       Eternity

                        Toi Ragland

* * *

Contents

• • •

Introduction

When I graduated from eighth grade I always wondered if I'd left a good impression on people, enough to remember me. High school and college were the same. Did I matter in people lives, I wondered? I wanted people to remember me. I'd hate to be that person to ask someone, "Do you remember me?" If so, what or why did they remember me? What was their memory of me? Which me did they know and remember? With many to choose from because I was a something else or at least I thought I was, I was curious to know, when were you apart of my life? It also would give me a chance to reflect on my past and appreciate my development as of today.

This book shows my growth. Growth that I am extremely proud of which took me only a few years compared to others lifetime. The rules became quite simple to me and I applied them vigorously. All the obstacles that I trialed through have become my strengths, my because and my reason why I am today. To me, it's a beautiful story of love, passion, and understanding self as well as others. I chose to do an Author's Elucidation at the end of each poem to explain a little about my actual thought process or my experience that lead me to writing each story.

* * *

Not only does it allow you to see and understand, clearly, my growth but it also helps you to not misinterpret what message I'm sending, which quite often happens when reading poetry.

Thank you for your support in choosing to listen to my words.

Enjoy

❋ ❋ ❋

BAD WAYS

Granny once spoke the words to me
"You shouldn't make everyone suffer because of one person"

Interpreting things differently
Not looking at what it really means
When taking it as you please you can really drive yourself to
an insanity coma

And like now, you can't remember that you were ever this
narrow minded which portrays an image of a child, trying to
retain your reason or what's left of it

Yet simultaneously feeling half way obligated to compensate
everyone around you, politely putting it "Kissing Butt"

Humph...now look at what this habit has developed while
standing in a pool full of self-inflicted pain

Momma warned you of your stubbornness and repeatedly
explained how it will hurt more than just you

Unmindful at that point what exactly those words meant
until now...
Now...I get it, you say

Oops..!?
Sarcastically speaking
My bad
True indeed...yeah, it's a bad inheritance from your dad is
where it started
But surely you're not mad
Cause you still intend to get exactly what you want
Until your bad ways catch up with you, I mean really catch up
with you

* * *

In which results to loneliness and bitterness with just the
walls to talk with

You'll remain the same and untamed
Cruel and your subconscious' fool
Not a dang thing will change

With a hand on your hip
A roll in your eyes
A suck of your teeth
And a tick in your neck

You give a piece of your mind one last time
And give it to them raw and uncut

"So if it's you who took a crash course in "Butt kiss 101" I'll
be nice and let you do the honors

❖ ❖ ❖

Edited more than twice, this poem was an angry writing. My Grandmother (Connie: RIP) told me on several occasions that when I get mad at one person I tend to make everyone suffer. She always said that when I got in that mood I was very unfair. In recollection, when I was about seventeen years old there was a huge devastation in my life and I took it out on EVERYONE. For whatever reason I was lied to about who my dad was and the man I knew to be my dad had just passed away. Second oldest of eight children, I ran to my big sis because although she knew of the truth prior to my knowledge, she was still my support system and I looked up to her tremendously in my teenage years. I abandoned my younger siblings and I didn't speak to my mother for months. I kept a distance from my grandmother because I knew she'd try to convince me to meet my biological dad. I gave into meeting him and said some awful things to him. I punished everyone who knew of this secret and also those who had no clue, all because of one person. Encountering plenty other circumstances, with different people I can remember getting the same response as what my grandmother told me. I was really good at holding a grudge and unfortunately I didn't care about anyone else's feelings because I unkindly thought of only myself. Because I was a victim, I played the victim.

The length I was capable of holding a grudge was something that my mother despised about me. I may still be a little stubborn sometimes but I don't hear it as much nowadays. In defense of my grudges, they only existed because I'd feel an apology was needed or things needed to be discussed and not swept under the rug. I needed time to understand things about myself and whomever I held the grudge with (like my mother for example) so I wouldn't

* * *

speak to the offending person until I was good and ready. In my mothers' case it took me three to four months to say anything to her because she lied to me. She and her secrets on top of my dad's death and just being a teenager almost caused me not to graduate from high school because all of this happened the second semester of senior year and I didn't know how to take it. I wanted her to tell me why, say "I'm sorry" and understand the pain she caused and she needed to take that first step, not me. The type of family I grew up in, the adults had no reason to explain anything to kids, so I didn't get what I wanted. Over the course of time I forgave her, accepted who she was and came to agreement that she probably felt she did no wrong. Even years later, after making few attempts to talk to her about it (after I'd silently forgiven her for the sake of forgiveness) she would still ignore me. Due to that dreadful year with my mother, graduating, the loss of my dad, a gain of a new dad, and no explanation from my mother I was a despicable and bitter person for a long time...seven years to be exact. I allowed my mother's action to influence me in a negative manner, I was infected. My dad had his explanations but I was angry with him too. Eight years after the incident at the age of twenty-five my mother poured her heart out to me and said, "I'm sorry". That was the first time I ever heard her say those words. My soul was bearing a weight I wasn't sure I'd ever recover from but when she said those words I felt I could get and have anything I wanted if I just be patient. But yes, I was mad and felt the world owed me something and I wasn't kissing any ass to get what was destined for me. Silly teenager.

◦ ◦ ◦

CHECKMATE

When standing face to face and/or even side by side I get the
vibe that I'm in front of or beside myself
Noticing it may be some eerie stuff to say
But think of it as a mirror image, only not
Having managed my life in every relationship I finally had
things in a bag
Giving, but taking way more…mentally that is

Messed his head up and never let my guards down just like a
player would
But just as the saying, "I met my match"
He gave me a run for my money

The opposite sex, the reflection of me in him I see
Such a déjà vu type
Uh…this happened once before
Indeed it did
I'm the one who delivered it and now it's being delivered to
me

But who's to say who?
Speaking from first or second point of view
Is it me or you?
We're so much the same yet we're different
I see chess
You see a pimp theory
It's all a game that much is precise
With all due respect
You'll never win unless you gain mental control
Don't hate the player or the game
Despise yourself cause the jokes on you
Of course I know you, since you are me
Just in a different form, frame, and name

On a dark and light chess board, I'm the Queen

* * *

By all means I do as I please and get away with it
Allowing you to think you've cornered me in more ways than one
Shifting your focus completely on the outer me
Handing you enough rope to hang yourself
Before I blow your mind
Concentrating on what I might do, awaiting a slip move
Personally delivering me the key to unlock your door of agitation
Frustrated because you've contemplated way to long on me and not enough on you
I'm willing to take my time, no rush to commit just yet
Though when I do, it'll be my last
This Queen always wins
Game over Sweetie
That's checkmate

* * *

CHECKMATE

Author's Elucidation

Continuing my mean girl years, I now felt I'd experience more and I kept my guards up. I was in a weird relationship. An open relationship, mistress role, stupid role, but I was in love (I thought). I allowed myself to play second best and I ultimately was losing. I couldn't get what I wanted even though I was the sweet and nice girl for him/I still wanted more. I wanted to know there was more and I could have better from a man. But the problem was my mind, heart and actions weren't in sync. I was in love and pissed that I was settling for less. So I made a decision and I wasn't going to lose.

Once I mastered my strategy, I committed myself to making him love me more. And once I did, I'd hurt him just as he tore my heart. I was out for revenge. Sad but true. I was going to give him a relationship kill 'em with kindness.

Oddly at the same time, I was just learning how to play chess. About three times a week I would play with anyone who visited me and recognized the Queen moves as correspondence with how I needed to be in order to become successful at accomplishing this goal. The Queen is just bad!

Day after day I put a lot of energy into making sure it worked, so it had to work. It didn't back fire either because I was determined not to lose. I grew a black heart for him and I was obsessed with the energy shift I'd developed. I still adored him but he had no idea. He chased me for a long time and I loved having him eat out the palm of my hand. I bet to this day he still thinks I was being mean to him because I was mad at him. In all honesty, I slipped into a psychotic mode of loving the torture when the initial goal was to wing myself from a bad drug because I was addicted to being his mistress.

❀ ❀ ❀

Unfortunately, I misused some really good energy on nonsense.

. . .

AS WE SEE IT

All hope is lost for the ones I hoped for
All hope is lost for the ones I hoped for

Now witnessing repetition, I speak on three
One man maybe two in hopes of approaching three
Or maybe one in approaching of two becoming three

Whatever the case they have a destiny or had it for that
matter
And just when a fork is formed they choose the wrong-left

All hope for whom?
All hope for me, the woman in search of a genuine man

Possessing morals
With boundaries
Obtaining pride of where he comes from
Nor city or state
But the woman who holds a covenant

All hope is lost
Sorry to say
But the world that we live in is the day before yesterday
replayed today
NO ONE LEARNS

● ● ●

This poem is one of many reasons I decided to do an author's elucidation. Strictly because there can be very different meanings when pertaining to more than one opinion and in today's world people misinterpret everything on purpose just to cause drama and controversy. So I'm making an attempt to nip that in the bud.

I've experienced and witnessed men that I love and those, whom I don't know very well, continue to disrespect their mothers. Whether it was face to face or behind their backs, it was done. Not being grateful or showing gratitude of the strength of their mothers. Consciously and subconsciously these men are adding to the disrespect for all women that we see in relationships and marriages. Having an influence as a friend, sister and a young woman I felt obligated to make an attempt to help my generation and children's generation as well by helping the men around me who are struggling with respecting their mothers. Help them to understand their mistakes and lack of love. I got down to the soul reason for these unkind acts towards their mothers and begged them to look on the brighter side. I begged them to take the blame and forgive and respect. At the same time, I felt hope was lost because they weren't willing to change and accept it for what it was. They will infect the next generation and the cycle will continue until someone learns to get out of their own way and change for something greater. Fast forward, then I prayed for them.

• • •

YOURS AND MINE

Sunrise and Sunset
Before work and especially after work
During lunch and brunch
Mingling and or socializing
Converting and not conversations

My expressions give me away
With my eyes opened and my ears unbolted

One minute after midnight and two minutes after noon

When I'm grown and on my own
Nevertheless, you're twelve or twenty-one

Inside or outside
Public or private
If you're inbounds or out
And its' your point or mine
Regardless if it's your info or mine
If I have a family or not
My business is mine and what's yours is yours

* * *

I was becoming extremely annoyed with the disrespect that was going on in my family. Because I was one of the few who didn't care what I said, so long as it was the truth, I didn't mind hurting your feelings if it took that for you to get it through your head. I very seldom just shut my mouth. Figuring that because we are family, I had the right to butt in, I continued to do so when I felt it was needed. I despised seeing someone being attacked because of a bad choice they made, yet I attacked the attacker because of their choice to attack. I was despicable. I assumed I was better than the other person because I was actually trying to better them and their current circumstance though on the other hand they felt the agony of being attacked by me. There was a guard up and I got caught in the middle. Quite often I did this. I defended with a beneficial intent so much, I couldn't count them all even if I wanted to. More often than wanted I'd end up being in the middle of chaos. With growth and time, I learned that I was wrong. I learned it's best to stay out of people business especially if its family. Give advice only when asked your opinion and even then be kind. Listen and understand the different point of views, never judge the heart and mind or make any assumptions. My mother, grandmother, aunts, uncles, or any adult for that matter would always say to the children, "Speak only when spoken to." Now once again that phrase has a new meaning to me.

* * *

BONDING

He felt it
He really did
Although I knew he always did
He tried not to show it
You may look at him brand new
I might think less of him
His friends are going to clown him
But he felt it and he revealed it and he released
The hurt, pain and sorrow
He's pleading for forgiveness
His joy, his happiness, his future
With or without
Sensitivity lies behind all his pride
Loyalty lies within his muscles
Dignity rolls off his tongue
And I saw it all
No need to speak, couldn't do it, even if he tried
Can't figure where to start
So he showed me instead
Through his facial expressions, his gestures, and the depth of
love in his eyes
When they were clear of tears, I saw it
Then he held his head close to his heart
As I stared at the back of his head
Ashamed....maybe?
I could hear his thoughts through his body language
I heard his sacred thoughts through his soul
Comprende'
And when I held him close to me, he saw me
My soul, my thoughts, he heard my forgiveness
Just in the nick of time
In the tick of time
A boy turned into a man
For that night he cried out to me
Not inside
But out loud

* * *

BONDING

Author's Elucidation

A man I know was at a crossroad in his life that forced him to make a move onto a new because his old life was verbally, mentally, and financially abusive. He developed a love and bond with a boy child and called him his own. Starting from the baby's third or fourth month of life this man was there to be his father figure. After several years of being there for this child, leaving his old life to begin a new life was extremely hard for him. He missed this child very much and after confiding in me, I thought he was just making excuses to go back to his old lifestyle due to it being financially easier. But he genuinely cared about the young boy. He informed me of the love he had for him and how hard life had become without the young child in his life. My dear friend would also make visits to the school to see the young boy and try to let him know he was still there for him. He would give him money and gave him his cell phone number, just in case the boy needed to talk. A year after the whole ordeal and months of no contact with him, they drifted apart. The man then had a child of his own in his new relationship. Unfortunately, he felt he was destroying this little boys' life because he was the male figure and the positive force in his life and now he was abandoning someone he truly loved. He was really fighting himself. And when he cried for the love of a child that wasn't his, he was embarrassed but at that very moment I witnessed the birth of a man.

* * *

PUPPY LUV

Wayyyy back when in ancient years
Was around the time I first set eyes on you
Barely making ten you had me in a daze
Too shy to say what I wanted to say
Because your appearance took my breath away
It was puppy love but in dog years I still got time

Couldn't make it official too many disagreements
I still remember the way it felt when you touched
my.....mmmm
Not going over board because I was a young thang, sweet
thang, a sensitive thang
It was a low down shame the way I played with your mind
Did you mine?
It was puppy love but in dog years I still got time

Remembering the first date and gift
Theater movie and jewelry with your initial
The first, second, and third break up and make up to you,
sweetie is what I really wanna do
It was puppy love but in dog years I figure, I still got time

Time goes by and by and by and by
I see you maturing now even more appealing than before
Wanting that first kiss after nine long anxious years
I intend to fulfill you my dear
Just to satisfy you as my man
I know it was dog years but in that case I still got time

I think I needed some sort of challenge or competition to
prove to myself you were
Naw, you are the man that I need
The man that completes me
And just to see you with another makes me lust for no other
Is she who I'll ever be?

* * *

It was puppy love but in dog years I know I still got time

Sweetie you don't understand were supposed to be my man,
my first in love
My everything with no regrets
You're not by my side just yet so I know I got work to do
My love because in dog years I still got time
I won't rush because I'm already claiming what's mine

⬥ ⬥ ⬥

PUPPY LUV
Author's Elucidation

Do you remember when you had a puppy love? He or she may have been the most appealing thing you'd ever set eyes on, during those times. You probably fell head over heels about that person. Little love notes, candy, jewelry from the bubble gum machine? I know you remember that, right? And then years after development you begin to reminisce. That was me. I had this one fellow that I was crazy about and I think the feelings were mutual. We couldn't be around each other for more than five minutes without a burst of an argument. I later found out he was in a relationship and the woman he was with wasn't what I thought she should be, maybe because she wasn't me. Oddly though, I really didn't want him because I knew it would never work, I still enjoyed seeing him drool over me even when she was around. Yeah, I was a monster, young, beautiful, and a true force to be reckoned with, in my earlier years. I didn't hurt her (I don't think that I did), just wanted to have fun and she had very little to do with my fun. I still wanted our innocence we shared so it didn't go further than a kiss. But that kiss was worth the nine year wait. He'll always be my puppy luv and that's all.

* * *

SERENDIPITY

I'm hearing a soft sound
Instruments maybe-music from heaven
A voice
A wonderful/beautiful voice
A voice I haven't heard in quite some time
Passionately
Sings
To me

A gentle touch..of a hand to another
A tingling stroke....of a hand to another
A sweet kiss.... from one to another hand

Other than the words of the song
No words are being exchanged
Telling everything there is to know
Of thoughts
Being thought
By both
Reading between the lines

The feeling...
This feeing was so real
So real yet surreal and dreary like
Like I was flying in the moment
With the birds and the stars
With the clouds and the angels

A quick glance signifies
An inner understanding and connection
I taste the hunger in your eyes
I'm floating on cloud 9
Watching the time pass me by

● ● ●

While the music crescendos
While the pitch gets higher
While the glance momentarily becomes a stare
The music has taken control of me
While staring with "Dead Silence"
While sharing cheek brushes with "Dead Silence"

A blank page
A page with
No thought…
No feeling…
No expression…
No emotion…
No sight?…
No sight…
No sound, with…
"DEAD SILENCE"
Now that's love

This is something
I hear
I see
There is emotion
There is expression
I know my feelings
I know my thoughts

Though I am completely mystified, I know
I continue to fly within those moments
And that's what I call serendipity

＊ ＊ ＊

SERENDIPITY
Author's Elucidation

How many times have you and a special someone sat and listened to the radio and a song came on that explained your emotions and thoughts for that person? At that exact moment you feel like the artist is singing directly to you, watching you even with each lyric he/she has hit the nail on the head. That happened to me before on more than one occasion, however this particular time I decided to write about it because I was left feeling the bliss of surrealistic moments.

We both had a bit of vocal skills and would often sing to each other, corny I know. I remember not seeing him for a while and one day he just popped up at my house. I sat in the car with him and we talked. (I believe he played the song for me instead of it playing on the radio) I knew the words to the song but never put much thought into them until he began to sing them to me. Every word was dead on. He serenaded me with his voice, Musiqsouldchild's lyrics to LOVE. So I understood the song on that day, if not any other day before. Most of the poem is about the beautiful sound of the actual song, until something else was taking place in the physical form. This guy wasn't someone I considered myself to be in love with, because once again, I didn't let it get that far. However, when we were together we had a blast. I know what you're thinking. Of course he wanted more...don't they all? At the end of the song, he told me the reason for popping up at my house and the serenading. He was attempting to butter me up for something, right? He had a baby boy! Go figure.

* * *

WATCHING YOU

Beside you as we lay
I stare
I take my time, a risk of losing sleep to admire the one beside
me
With love on my mind, I smile
I close my eyes and let my hand remember your structure,
For the times we are apart
Or maybe for the elder years
That I won't get lonely at night
Your comfort elites me
Your scent relaxes me
Should I place my hand upon you
I wait
To listen for your subconscious respond that eases me
Gently removing the wrinkles from your forehead
With a rub of my thumb
Tempted to kiss you, though I wait
Readjusting for comfort allows the perfect timing to grab
spoon to you
Blissfully insane over you
I noticed that when I caught myself watching
In amazement as you sleep

* * *

WATCHING YOU
Author's Elucidation

Not to come forth with a crazy approach but have you ever watched someone while they slept? A baby, spouse, or loved one? Someone who you've felt a piece of serenity when you watch them? The body subconsciously responds to you and/or to your voice. A baby for instance, sometimes when you stroke them while sleeping (if they are familiar with your touch) they will smile and that is priceless. Ever notice if you go to sleep upset with your spouse that there isn't any touch, not so much as a pinky toe on your leg. And how dare you actually make contact on accident, you are almost certain to an aggressive jerk away, signifying, "I'm still mad at you, so don't bother me." And that's all while the other is asleep! On the other hand, you have a pleasant evening and the body responds in a more relaxed manner. Sometimes if you're lucky you can get the subconscious to verbally respond, those who talk in their sleep. To me, it is self-comforting to observe the behavior of loved ones while sleeping, while dreaming. It's all out of love.

* * *

BE PATIENT

What a shame how I continue to search for Mr. Right and
have yet to find him
Is he you, my friend?
Fully aware of the circumstances I'd bring upon myself
The kiss of death, he has concealed himself in a gentle form
I've died and gone to heaven
But hey, let's not get too emotional here
Explaining to me...
Darling I really
Darling we can
Honey you should
And
Yes Baby let's
But I don't want to crush you with infidelity
Though should you require that much from me there's no
need for infidelity
Why wait?
Now it's said that good things come to those who wait
While you dismiss your Misses and the Mrs.
So you can be completely committed to me
And who's to say you're what's good for me?
La la de da
So we meet again, not thinking very clearly just looking into
your innocent eyes and going with the flow
Any time any place I don't care who's around but no one's
around
Now look at what we have here
Entrapment
Body speaking to me in a language I'm not used to
Yet I won't allow it to override one's ability to think before
doing things
Everything about you impels me to a foolish morale
I want to be ready but I'm stuck at the starting line
So I'll wait

● ● ●

I'll wait for you, for me, a ring
And you think I don't mean it but yes, "I DO"
Cause good things do come to those who wait
Just be patient and you'll get what's coming to you

* * *

BE PATIENT

The peer pressure that we endure as adolescence and adults is a tremendous obstacle that affects everyone at some point in our lives. Sex and drugs are main topics when discussing peer pressure. In this poem and in my mind of adolescence, I had to tap into my roots in order to stay strong and be firm with my decision. My reasons why were mainly the opposite of what had become an epidemic. I wanted to be one of the very few girl(s) in high school, in my class, who actually had morals. I thought it was better to stay pure than saying I was with Joe over the weekend and "Girrrrrrl let me tell you!"

Many guys knew of my purity and I didn't mind because I was a proud virgin. Dating here and there but not letting it get too far. I believed at one point the boys had a bet on me, I'm sure they did, that's just what boys do. As expected, I ran across some smooth talkers too, well dressed, good looking, and educated. The top of the class even…. Yes?! Boy was I tempted but ultimately I gained respect. Though at times when I would be around everyone who was "getting down", I didn't know their language or their jokes because I still had my innocence. I never let it bother to me because I knew that what I was doing was right. I had self-control and I remained patient.

❋ ❋ ❋

YOU TOLD ME

Having unaccountable sleepless nights (previous to this one)
When I cry to myself
Not understanding
Why
When
Where
Who
and how could you leave me all by myself on this night of joy
Alone I stand
What did I do to deserve this sentence?
This cruelty
This abandonment from you that I never expected
Allowing you to hurt me consistently I played the fool for
you, LOVE, who don't love me
Trying to justify who exactly let you into my heart
Because to the obvious mind a barbed wire fence would be
the best protection
Charming, Prince Charming you
Having cried out all the tears I could cry for you
Now I'm finished, it over, that's it, that's all
This is the last of my confusions and discombobulating
frustrations
With us, with you, with her, with this
Simple inquires being left unanswered as if you are now
some sort of mime or the hearing impaired
Yet when an attempt is made you speak in fragments, in code
Code to who?
No need to spare my feelings now
The damage has been done
Soft yes but not fragile
The healings of a wound come in due time
Ooh
But Nanna never warned me about these times and men like
you we never discussed

＊ ＊ ＊

Don't you remember you told me you love me?
Love me....
I know love isn't supposed to hurt
So from now on I choose your love no more

YOU TOLD ME
Author's Elucidation

Being in a relationship is hard. Being in a
relationship, while playing the third wheel, is even harder.
Naturally people get greedy and selfish when they can't
decide what they want. Ever been stood up before? How
about being stood up on a very special occasion? It's really no
fun at all. Emotions begin to run like crazy with one hundred
questions to follow. Realizing that you deserve better, you
start to wonder, how did it even get to this point? Why did I
let myself get hurt? Something about he/she was just as
suave as can be or either you were weak, vulnerable at the
time. After you get a chance to calm down and get the
courage to ask why, they all of a sudden have selective
hearing but want to smooth talk you and try to comfort you
with a less likely meaningful "I'm Sorry". Growing up boy or
girl, we've all heard stories about the heart breaks in detail
and some not so detailed. I guess we never quite understand
until we go through it ourselves. To choose not to support
that kind of love is brave, healthy and a great start to
understand who you really are.

＊ ＊ ＊

VICTIM

Heard the stories
Women vs. men version
Even had the opportunity to hear from the horse himself
Each seemed to be as accurate as accurate can be
But I never thought I'd be a victim of your love

Never witnessed an ordeal as such
Never even wanted to see, not so much as a peek
Always heard but never listened
A hard head makes a soft... you get the point
Now I'm a victim of your love, I've witnessed

Or is it?
Do you really?
What seems to be a stupid question to you
Is a jigsaw puzzle to me and I've missed the clue
Abuse I hear
I feel abused
Your love I hear
I feel no truth
So I'm a victim of your...what?

Words maybe
It gets much deeper than that
Evaporation of the mind notice the repetition of thoughts
I feel it be
I am a victim of your words indeed

A victim that I am
Maybe not like the others
In which I've casted this upon myself
Better off as a witness
I wouldn't have mind
But I'm a victim of your something
Trying to get free

* * *

Everyday women and men, even children, are becoming victims of verbal, mental, and physical abuse. Verbal and mental abuse can often be worse than physical abuse because the mind has the ability to shut down the body. It's easier to heal the body than the mind because the mind is a file cabinet full of memories which generally acts and responds to experiences. When the brain remembers something in detail it causes a reaction.

What can make the situation tough is longing for the love from the abuser. In most cases the attacker doesn't feel like they really did anything wrong, they were provoked and should they feel remorse then it's kept a secret from the victim. So they continue to ignore or try to forget what happened, don't want to talk about it. Forbidding the conversation be brought up then that rage and anger flares up again.

I remember when I was a child (k-6) I was bullied quite often, I was a cute kid with awkward features. My head, hands, and feet out grew me and I was skinny. Though I was smart it just wasn't enough for the kids to leave me alone. I'd go home to my mother and cry to her about my bad day and what the kids said to me. She'd always tell me, "sticks and stones may break my bones but words would NEVER hurt me". It didn't take long for me to realize that was just a saying to strengthen me. That phrase wasn't true at all. In fact, words hurt you the most when you don't have a clue and when you are focused on the wrong words because they are filed away in your recollection labeled "about me", with potential of causing internal damage if you allow it to. And at some point we all are trying to break free of someone's harsh

● ● ●

word choices that were once spoken to us. There is power behind a word but it's our responsibility to condition the mind through the challenging times.

* * *

TOUCH OF A MAN

Touch of a man
That man with the touch
I felt he placed his hand on me
Touched real deep, inside my heart
I felt him even in my dreams
He made me a distant shade of misty blue
He completely took my breath away
I felt his hands as they compressed my face
Strong masculine arms he held firmly around my body
What a man he is
What a touch he has
I pray and I ask
Is this what I prayed for?
That look he gave me as he stared deeply into my eyes
Lifting me higher than ever before
I see his muscles going to use
Holding my arms so tightly
Making sure I didn't move
On top of me now in a different position than before
He showed me his love as we rolled around on the floor
Didn't last very long but nothing ever does
This man gave it to me raw and uncut
What you see is what you get
He showed me his heart and I peeked into his mind
The touch of a man, it was, that drove me
He captivated my heart and disciplined my mind
He took over my body
It was no longer mine
I learned to love his touch
I hated to love his touch, is what made me decide that I was
his property and in no one else I could confide
He helped me to diminish my self-esteem
He was to do, damn well what he pleased
Rather he piss on me than mentally rape me

• • •

But what a man he is
Even taught me how to cover girl
I applied and lied
I omitted
And gave no more than required
Sometimes when I look at him I see the man that touched me
like no other
Besides the fact, I plaster my mouth and anchor my tongue
because his words are taint and brawny yet his touch is
stronger

* * *

TOUCH OF A MAN
Author's Elucidation

The touch of a man took my friend away from me, momentarily. In my teenage years, a dear friend of mine and I would see the billboards about domestic abuse to young women and teenage girls who were in those type of relationships. These girls would have black, blue even swollen eyes and the billboard would read, "He's really sorry this time". We'd always talk about how dumb these girls were to stay in the relationship and get beaten up. She and I agreed that it isn't that serious and that we'd never let a thing like that happen to us. Unfortunately, one of us didn't stick to that promise. I don't recall her ever having black eyes, maybe because it wasn't worth remembering, however I do recall an absence of her in my life. We lived fairly close to each other and I'd see her maybe once a week, we had small talk but wouldn't hang out anymore.

One day my sisters ran in the house to tell me that they'd just witnessed her get hit in the hallway of the apartment building. They begged me to help her but I didn't. I felt there was absolutely nothing I could do worth doing. I learned from my elder sister that it's unhealthy for you to get between a fight of a girlfriend of yours and her boyfriend. If I did help, one of two things would have happened, either she's get mad at me and attack me or he'd start hitting me just as he hit her. I wasn't too fond of neither happening to me so I stayed where I was. My little sisters were astonished. "When she's tired of getting beat, she'll leave him and I'll be right here waiting for her. But that's a battle I will not fight for her or anyone else because that's not my decision to put up with or not to put up with," I told my sisters. Though it did take her a while to get tired of the abuse, I was there when

* ◈ *

she was ready to talk. I love her now even more than I did back then.

I, on the other hand, was in a serious relationship and a buildup of frustration began with him and me. One day we were arguing and all of a sudden I became airborne. In attempt to throw me down some stairs, which didn't quite happen, he and I both began to go down while he was in a massive choke hold. (my military trained cousin taught me that grip) Terrified that I'd eventually have to let him go because he played football in school and I didn't want to kill him, after the release he hit me in my jaw. So hard that I thought it was on the right side of my face until the next day I woke up with the left side bruised and swollen. Don't get it twisted, I did my damage too while fighting back and he went home that night, all 400 miles give or take a few.

The difference with me was it took ONE time and that was it. If you ask him today if he'd ever lost a fight, he'll tell you, "Yeah, by a girl"! Am I proud of what I did? Indeed I am. Not that I hurt him but because I kept my promise to myself and didn't become a loves punching bag. It only took me one time to know that that wasn't what I wanted for myself in a relationship.

* * *

SHHH!!!!

Choosing to report undesired information upon no request is
a product of me overhearing unbarring criticism I really
don't need

Trying to admit to the one love of your life before he offers
his eternal proposal you saying yes undeniably

Understanding this is my choice of words
I wasn't told or questioned to tell my past
With Boo, Sweetie, Babe and Bay
I'm committed to you now I want this love to last
Exploiting personals about Bill and Tim was too bold and
cocky of me when you didn't even ask
Not forgetting about that one boy, little boy blue in the face
and Moe and Joe two friends now those days were a blast
And many other guys I choose not to mention only because of
long term memory lost and not enough tension

In your eyes you saw and see promiscuity

But I never said I revealed my naked truth to them

On the contrary I didn't say I didn't

So I'll leave you to assume the worst or the best

As much as I've ran my mouth
I think I've said enough and won't continue anymore
For the love of my life has renamed me Mrs. JoeBlow

As far as I'm concerned my eternal proposal no longer exists

Now see what happens when you try to come clean?
Your future has changes but your past remains the same

❀ ❀ ❀

So next time you feel the need to reveal just remember this
poem the title instills...
SHHH!!!!!!!!!!!!!!

· · ·

Having discussed this topic, among many other topics, with a host of girlfriends on separate occasions, I've discovered that many women more often than men, basically talk too much. Women talk too much about the little details in the relationship and men simply don't know how to act when questioned about the last woman. But I give most men credit, when credit is due; they aren't oozing with intimate details of the exes.

For whatever insecure reasons, women and men question the most recent significant other when entering a new relationship. They want to know what you've done, how many times, the last time and what happened with whom. Ultimately it really shouldn't matter because you fall in love with the person for the way they treat you and how well you react to each other. Not because of their past. If your past doesn't create a positive impact for your present/future relationship, then what's the use of sharing it? You'll love that person for who they are today and tomorrow. Should you feel the need to tell what happened in past relationships, never, I repeat, NEVER go into intimate detail especially if you see a possibility of a real future with this person. But also for yourself as well. Never reveal all your personal relationship history with anyone. Some things are better left unsaid; just keep it between you and God if it didn't involve that person. Sure if you've murdered someone or is an addict of substance abuse, sex, detrimental towards someone else's health or anything that would get you thrown in jail you may want to be honest. But if it's harmless to someone else and it was just an act of immaturity and you've grown, then just SHUT UP.

◦ ◦ ◦

TIMELESS

Timeless thoughts I cease yet to manage
Not comprehending the words spoken that comes from the
mouth of he
I don't know, I don't care, I can't, and I won't
Overwhelmingly too much negativity that exists from him

Timeless thoughts I cease yet to manage
With no precise vision to mention
Halfway intentions and failing to the idea of eventually
having to make a decision
So I say, think, feel, and subconsciously know
I don't know
Being selfish, to one individual that people say has a calling
for
Not appreciating life for a time practiced nor realizing these
obstacles are just tests
Having the urge of needing, wanting, feeling, and breathing
the air of no breath
Wanting nothing upon me but death

Timeless thoughts I cease yet to manage
To never manage
To overcome these imperious emotional phases and this long
term depression stage
Cry out for help but not eager to receive
Hey look, this is the perception I perceive
You having, self-pity, self-inflicted the pain you've excessively
endured
Finding weakness and hollowness in you because you see an
easy way out
If at first you don't succeed, try, try again

● ● ●

Timeless thoughts you continue to consume, I cease yet to manage
Full of exasperation, resentment, bemusement, mar and so afraid... of what?
Loss failure due to lack of communication and self-motivation allowing something
Non-excitant and past tense even to gain control of you in a doubtful intense manner
Living life not desiring a purpose

To whom it may concern, no I can't help
I really do feel I want a rebate
Being that I came a little too late
My attempted work is done because you my sweet, are apparently too far gone

• • •

Have you ever felt like you were stuck because of your situation, your choices? This poem was inspired by a beautiful spirited Christian woman who was my elder. We had a close relationship despite our differences in age and other personal vendettas. She'd experienced a great and tremendous loss of her husband. Soon after she re-married and didn't give herself time to miss, understand, and respect her late husband as a man, father, supporter and provider. The young children were devastated; their father was gone. Due to the sudden death of her husband she was compensated quite a bit.

Still resigning in her home, everything reminded her of her late husband so she moved out of that home and began a fresh start. Money was no object; therefore, she repeatedly spent loosely. Eventually, this woman remarried. Since she didn't build a good foundation with him in the beginning, her world was bound to crumble. She spoiled her new husband with the death offerings of her late husband. She now had become the sole provider. He failed to give her the motivation she was used to in as in her previous marriage. About five years into the new marriage everything took a turn for the worse. Her home was being foreclosed, with no place to live her husband began committing adultery and then he decided to leave her.

I'll never forget, I had an urge to call her for some reason that only God knows. We discussed a lot of things but once she began to speak about her unhappiness I went into a private room. Intimate things that I'd never thought she would reveal to me. And I even got a few words of encouragement in with her. Giving her my point of view on the outside looking in, she'd let herself go a bit. Although she went to church every Sunday, she was still focused on the wrong things and had little strength. That night we talked for nearly four hours. I talked the charge off my cell phone. Her time stood still while the world around her moved faster and faster. I'll never forget the special relationship we shared.

With Love and Respect, God Bless

● ● ●

AU' REVOIR

This is a true in depth psycho analysis on my emotions of
you...

You are my man, you were my man
Sweetie, in any definition it means the same
People change?
Yeah, so what!
Seasons change
When the suns sets the moon rises
And when it rains, a rainbow appears in the
aftermath
Big deal
You're a dog
At least that the manure my mom keep
feeding me
But in that case I'm a...
I think...
I don't know...
I'm confused, discombobulated, disoriented
Wow this is a bad bad misconception
I'm thinking I need a psychiatrist or hypnosis
Someone to trick me into believing I don't
want you
I'm having problems, situations and concerns
I'm on the verge of having an emotional crisis
Panic attack and nervous breakdowns
Ahhh!!!!
All this self-indulged psychological abuse is
kicking my butt
And miscellaneous crap must cease of having
self-pity and wanting comfort
Don't talk dim and gentle to me I need no
shoulder to cry on I have a sleeve
I need no hand to hold
Love me or leave me!

* * *

Better yet, love me by leaving me alone
Idiot
A hot gust of anxiety runs through my heart
because I find myself in the same
situation just with a different man, each and
every time
But he looks just like you
Different personalities
Now ain't that something
I realize life is simple but I'm the one who's
making it difficult
By allowing my obstacles to become a
derailment instead of detour
Which is you
I can go around you now because I know the less I get
attached to my surroundings the easier it is for me to get rid
of them

Now... what did you say your name was???

                                                                           * * *

My baby! This was the second poem I was extremely proud of. I'd act out this poem anytime I'd recite it to my friends, family and to myself in the mirror. I've never let anyone read it until now because I thought it was just too good to be read. In this period in my life I documented the step up of maturity I was blessed to gain and captured it with words. With the maturity now surfaced my poems gained their fair share also.

Addressing my emotions, the tone of this poem was pissed. I tried to do the long distance relationship with a love, while it was his first year in college. I knew what I was getting myself into so I agreed that whatever he does I would be fine with it because it was college. And everyone knows, in college, kids are getting a taste of life without the supervision of their parents so they often times let their hair down a bit. I wasn't afraid to have an open and honest relationship because I thought we had a good friendship first and foremost. Plus, I figured that's what I needed to do in order to keep a status. He didn't keep his part of the bargain. He was lying to me and anyone who knows me know that I despise a liar. He previously had developed a reputation but I thought since we had a friendship it would compensate and he'd have more respect for me. I felt betrayed and played with insanity because I was really trying to figure out where I went wrong. I named it Au'revoir because I was saying good-bye to the lies, him, insanity, and negativity. I wanted to hurt him but he would never let me recite the poem to him because it was bad talking him. Oh well, too bad because I think he would have loved it.

❋ ❋ ❋

THORN OF A ROSE

I grew a thorn and you never saw it coming
Right alongside the grooves of my hug
Symptoms upon arrival
He chose to ignore my voice of reason, my cry for help, my
whisper of serenity, and my signs of body language
So you couldn't understand my growing struggle from day to
day
The pressure just to be with you
You came down on me like the force of a wrecking ball

It was all a surprise to you
Huh?

Yeah
Everything is great, couldn't be better
Not bitter
Not angry
Do I still love you, yes I adore you
Even more when you bombard through the wall I built
I'll give you as you wish, in the way you've never seen
I grew a thorn and you never saw it coming

I needed you to feel the pain, real pain
To witness the insanity that Albert E spoke about
In which I dealt with when we spoke
I wanted to see my strength in you as you continued to
maintain your own independent strength
Hey, hey!
What are you doing?
You can't drop the ball...you told me that
Come on superman, I need to see our muscles now that I've
left with your backbone
The need to change and be appreciated is a must
And I see that happening once I learn to trust
And yes I did

* * *

That's the thorn I grew because it inflicted pain to you, to me,
because you continued to pick my roses
I had to do it for me and them
This mission was never about you
Though completely involving you
Healing upward the best of me

* * *

This poem was at the peak of my epiphany of life. I began to see the reasons why I had to do more, be more, have more and even give more. I use to complain about having too much to do for my house, children and job. Just made ample excuses why I couldn't reveal my potential to the world. I very often ranted about there not being enough time. Yet I wanted to be appreciated for being a wonderful housewife. "Shouldn't all that I do be enough", I questioned. I cooked, cleaned, did laundry, proactively schooled my children daily before they were old enough to attend kindergarten, had a nine to five, always looked presentable- as well as the children and saved money because I did everyone's hair (I was a license cosmetologist). I actually thought I was being Superwoman. Yet I still made excuses why I wasn't finding time for my craft. In a nutshell, I thought I was a trophy wife. (Stopped the partying, drinking, smoking and had God fearing morals) What more do you want from me? Right?

One day when watching an episode of Kimora-Life in the Fab Lane, I realized I hadn't scratched the surface of being a superwoman and a wonderful mother. Watching her maintain a great relationship with her children while continuing to build an empire revealed to me that she was a SUPERWOMAN and I wanted to do just that. (Maintaining well behaved children) If I didn't learn how to balance everything it takes to be a good wife and mother while still satisfying my passion while setting a good example for my children, then what exactly was I teaching them? I began to understand the importance of everything I did because my children are watching me. So I grew a thorn. I needed to be harsh to myself and my family every once in a while to show that commitment that I needed to achieve my goals.

* * *

My husband squabbled with me that it was easy to maintain balance. Only because he was without the children 70% of the time, I made it easy for him. I wanted him to appreciate me. Nevertheless, I couldn't understand that in order for him to appreciate me I had to reveal that talent he saw hiding in me. Eventually I began to blossom like a flower. So thank you SugarB and Kimora Lee.

* * *

COLORFUL WISHES

I sit upon the mist of a wishing well
Discovering the epitome of delightfulness at the presence of
dreaming water
So many wishes to be made without a jingle of change

No pennies, nickels, quarters or dimes
Just a bag full of skittles with rattles of chimes
Red, yellow, purple, orange and green, will have to do

So I pray over these candies as it to add value
Proceeding to drop them one by one with a sweet wish
behind them for me and you

Wishing for love- the color was red, filled with passion, fire
and lots of desire
Yellow was next and I wished for the best
Eternal beams of brightness from the sun with an everlasting
perfect sight

Purple, which is my favorite of all
Wished that all my good dreams would come true

The spice of life which I need in my repertoire
I wished as I aggressively tossed the orange right in

Now green left me confused
I stumbled about
So I wished that this feeling I would not be without

Five colorful wishes I've made at this well
With distinctiveness please come true with skittled coins

• • •

COLORFUL WISHES
Author's Elucidation

This poem was inspired by a child I saw sitting at this giant water fountain (it wasn't really huge, the child was just rather small) eating skittles. Other children had come to the fountain and made their wishes with coins. But when he asked his mother for some change she said, "Sorry honey I don't have any more money. I spent my last on the skittles you're eating". "But Mommy I have to make a wish", the young boy replied. At that moment I could just read the hurt on his mother's face because she really didn't have it. I checked my purse and of all the times I have change, this time I had not one penny. Seeing all the other children so joyously tossing their coins in the fountain, he made a decision to not leave without making his wishes.

He grabbed a skittle of every color and closed his eyes. One by one I witnessed him toss the skittles in just as though they were coins. His mother observed in silence while her heart seemed to become at peace. I was graced by a four or five-year-old little boys' determination rise and become innovative. Skittles in a fountain? He also made a small sacrifice. I thought it was really sweet because after he was done he said to his mother with a huge smile on his face, "I hope that works!" So the next time you see strange things in a fountain, it's probably because Mommy or Daddy didn't have any change and that child had to make a wish regardless of what it was with.

* * *

DREAMING REALITY

Walking in the footsteps of what they call reality
Sleeping in the world they say is dreaming
When only months ago seems like last week I realized that
time flies tremendously
Not waiting for me nor you
Just like a dream everything happens so fast in such little
time with no room for miscalculation
And last night I dreamed of your face

Walking in the footsteps of what I think is a dream
Sleeping in the world of what some say is reality
Please tell me which is which
For what reason do we déjà vu
This happened before, don't you agree
Could I have saw this happening before it really hit reality
A dream
You're the one I had reality about or dreamed about for that
matter
The tone reminded me, your baritone chilled my skin

Walking in the footsteps of what I hope is a dream
Sleeping through the world they say is reality
Distinguishing no difference of which is which
In reality I know I don't belong
Though in reality I dream I do
Please let this be a dream so therefore I can choose not to
wake
You'll desire my touch making it easier for you to identify
Relaxing your mind for whatever this dream has to offer
What you see is what you get
Too good to be true
You dream what is reality
Should it be, could it be, that I'm dreaming
Pinch me quick
Cause I'm walking in the footsteps of what they call reality
But feels like a dream

* * *

And sleeping in the world of what they say is dreaming
But feels like reality
Unable to decipher the difference whenever we're as one
Heaven never ends and ecstasy prolongs for infinity
Because I'm sleep walking with my eyes wide open and
getting lost in time
Concluding in terms this is what
I call dreaming reality

DREAMING REALITY
Author's Elucidation

Have you ever had a dream that felt awfully real? Then you wake up, right? Well that happens to me very often and then I wake up and wake up again. I've had dreams inside dreams. But the most fascinating dream I've had is the one that I'm in now. Many times the world around me is so unbelievable that I wish it were a dream. Other times it essentially feels like a dream. What would happen if the two worlds collide, reality and dreaming, I asked myself? So I began to feel good in reality just as I would in a dream to help make my dreams come true. And I started with the man of my dreams as a test to myself. After a few prayers to God I began to visualize his face.

I have déjà vu quite frequently. More than I would think is normal. But what exactly is normal and do I want to be? Believe it or not I enjoy getting déjà vu so often because it's confirming the stars are in alignment for me. It enlivens me because I always feel like something great is about to happen due to other positive events in my life.

Night after night I would have terrible dreams. Afraid to fall asleep with engagement of reoccurring nightmares I resorted to deleting certain things I watched on television. Once the dreadful dreams where gone I grasped the concept of having good dreams come from having good days, weeks, and thoughts of peace, love and forgiveness. And I redefined my living as dreaming reality.

* * *

MUTED

As still as I can be
I stand alone quietly
Finding that special place inside myself I've learned to enter
when the world around me turns to chaos
So motionless
I can feel the blood as it flows through the main artery of my
neck
Temperature now arising causes a slight jitter within the
bloods rhythm like boiling water
Rushing to the top of my body trying to find an escape route
An instant headache

The pace of my heart has now become as rapid as the beat of
a newborn
Expressing my feelings
Explaining my actions
Understanding my troubles
Reclaiming my spotlight
Exhilarating my peacefulness
Exercising my respectfulness among the elders
Exfoliating the washed up outer me
I've politely revealed the new and improved me
The empowered and more in tuned she

As I've refreshed the skin I'm in
No one has shared my exultant happiness
Have you heard a word that I've said?
That I'm saying?

Tapping into that special place once more to regain, rejoice,
rebirth, rebuild me
Out of breath, no words left
I've shared my peace and you don't hear
I've screamed

* * *

I've shouted
I've jumped and pouted
Yet you can't hear me since you've muted my happiness

Unaware of my existence so how could you hear the lioness
roar
Now immune to the sweet divine sound of my whisper
Why would you dare to pay attention?
So oblivious to the monotone passion that I speak from
within
When should you listen then?
Who?
Yes, you and you and you
She-him-her-he and you too
Everyone has crowded me to see why it is that she doesn't
speak
You choose to turn my volume down because I hear me loud
and clear
For those who have cast out my voice as I speak
And neglect to understand the words as I teach
I shall pursue a new approach to maintain my peace
As my words are dear now read them and weep

● ● ●

Have you ever been in the state of mind where the only thing you could say was, "I'll be damned"! That's the "be damned" state of mind because you've found a new meaning to something that you've used in a different way. That's exactly how I felt in this poem. At my happiness point in my life (thus far) I rejoiced to everyone that I finally understood life. I told them I know why people say things like, "You have so much potential and follow your heart and put God first". Things I've heard all my life and that so many of us have heard; now I understand what they really mean. I tried to explain it to my loved ones but they couldn't realize what I was saying because they didn't open up and simply it wasn't their time. They didn't want to believe in change, no matter how young or old they were. My language was crazed and deranged, "Is everything okay with her, is she sick and about to die", they thought. Smirking as if I'd lost my mind. "Well I'll believe you when you get there", it was told to me. And I always thought to myself that of course you'll believe it then because it will be visible to you. Bad thing is I won't share the same joy when I get it because I was expecting it. Be really happy for me now and later...not just later.

Telling people you've really changed is like an addict checking out of rehab early. They're waiting for you to relapse. I tried several different attempts and no one got it. People hear what they want to hear because they don't want to know you're doing better for yourself or better than them so they put you on mute. But I don't want to be better than anyone, let's be great together. Friends and family started to question one another about the behavior they saw in me, thinking I needed help or it's me searching for help. That's the part that caused me to feel like a pot of boiling water because I had to bite my tongue. So this poem was actually

* * *

my final attempt to tell them that I understand life and they should too. Can you hear me now? Good.

● ● ●

BEAUTIFUL MINDED

When happiness should burst out of me I exude sadness
Understanding plenty yet lacking wisdom
Which makes no sense being that you gain wisdom from
understanding
Then why do I consume the feeling of ignorance
So rich yet poor in other aspects
Very thankful but search for reasons to complain
Full on occasions but hunger for more
Everyone wants happiness conveying a global search
Disputing the fact that happiness will come to you
Getting all side tracked so engaged to witness the ultimate find
Needing it to last forever more knowing nothing ever will
Without happiness life become chaotic
Our actions become violent towards each other and
unfortunately ourselves
The innocent become victimized
Paranoia develops
When holding what used to be a typical conversation you
accuse its patronized
Delusional thoughts that no one cares
Neglecting to mention its self who cares less
Due to yourself indulged mental abuse
When happiness and joy is present you disburse a frown
Jealousy is provoked
Arguing with voices not realizing there's no face
There's a brawl taking place
You against you
One glance in the mirror now the voices have a face
Thinking deeper and deeper has tortured you so
On a downward spiral to the bottom of the barrel
Reaching for someone to grab on to on your way down

* * *

A beautiful mind, that's what it is
You've tormented yourself when you chose to find happiness
instead of letting happiness find you

* * *

This poem shows a contradiction of thoughts, feelings, and actions. Many people often feel and think one emotion but show something the exact opposite. We find reasons to complain about and make excuses why we don't have and our focus shifts on the negative. Doing this is actually a fight with yourself that takes place whenever your thoughts aren't cohesive with your feelings and actions. Under seeing that you have become your own greatest obstacle, you are now standing in your own way. A downward spiral of negative thoughts is born. When insanity meets insanity the outcome can be very violent. There's violence among you and the innocent by standers, noting there will always be innocent by standers because misery loves company.

I believe, the absence of love and God in your life causes (or helps contribute) to the self-mutilation. Sometimes loneliness can take place as the result of delusional thoughts, constructing an isolated box around you, which is the perfect recipe for self-mutilation. Some keep it simple by reverting back to the beginning and reapplying one's self and it works for them. However, when there is complexity, simplicity has no surviving chance. So, we dig deeper and deeper in search of what we believe is the correct answer, with potential of self-destructing the mind. A beautiful mind can be in two different forms; the peace you find in simplicity- applying what was taught in childhood years or the ability to single handedly destruct the mind by involving complexity- when you allow your adult experiences to blur your vision of simplicity.

* * *

ME AND SHE

She told me to do it
So I hope you miss me a little bit when I leave
The simple girl in my head said
You said NO
She said GO
She told me to dismiss all commotion
Though I can complicate it so
When I evaluate my reasons why
I stay
I cry
A part of me continues to die

She told me to do it
You'll be pissed when you notice that you missed
The ten-year-old fearless little girl inside
I said wait
She said to
Not me
Under the influence I try to fight her then
But she comes to my defense even more when
.12 DWI indeed
She speaks to me
Rare

So explicit she told me to do it
She'll never leave me
Influenced or not
Yet she loves me more at when
Let's win she said
I said
We said
They'll get it when we are created recreated by self
Myself a new

* * *

She told me to do it
So I did
She's got my back
She holds my strength
Gives me my sanity and glee
Don't miss me when I'm gone
Celebrate when I return

* * *

When was the last time you got a break? I mean a real break. You ever just wanted time to yourself, away from the kids, spouse, friends, family and strangers? Just alone in peace to ponder your next move. To anyone who has little ones, it is important to get that break to regroup.

Well I felt like that plenty of times and I thought it was wrong but I realized that I really deserved it. When I didn't get the break I wanted, I felt like just running away. I felt like running away from my family just because I felt overwhelmed with my wife and motherly duties. Often times I would get so consumed with the needs of my family that I forgot I had friends. I was a mother of a one-year-old and a five-year-old in kindergarten. Part time school bus driver in which my one-year-old could ride along, writing a book, still at the epitome of my understanding of life, God, relationship battles, a part of building our business and the standard everyday concerns. I had a plate that was too full and my appetite didn't correspond. Whatever the case, 90% of the time I had at least one of the children with me. We had no babysitters, no money, and no time for ourselves to enjoy each other's company. I started thinking, "What if I left for a while and didn't say anything to anyone, who would I blame it on"? But I'll be back and ready to continue. My husband looked at me like I lost my mind and gave me a hug. He kissed me on my forehead and told me, "How about you get one weekend each month by yourself instead"? It was a great gesture and I agreed to it but have yet to get even one weekend to myself. But that's okay.

❋ ❋ ❋

ESCAPING

Your perception of life is so remarkably distant from actual reality it leaves me often to wonder if I'm in this world alone, if my vision is singled out and no one else sees nor understand my sight

Your choice of words apparently not clearly organized is so annoyingly perplexed that even if I wanted to I couldn't comprehend which leaves me wondering in a world of fluster Stuck on an island of working motor boats but can't move

Every word that describes confused is precisely how I feel and this feeling is real
This I know isn't a dream because I frequently experienced these emotions wanting to escape wishing I were someone else or something else other than me

Because I'm often afraid, terrified, petrified of words, I want to be the lion off the Wizard of Oz wanting courage only to find that I already have it, but where is it, someone must have hidden it

If I were invisible it would be perfect that way no one would see me to spit at me or look at me differently, I can see you but you can't see me

If I were a rock the whole object would be for me not to feel at all because even love hurts

If I were a radio that would be just what I need, that way at least someone would be listening to me

If I were water I'd wash away all life distortions I have; clean I would be

* * *

A bird to fly away from any situations I don't like, just move elsewhere

Where is it, someone had to hide it all
My pride, my dignity, courage and strength everything that makes me a woman

If I were you and you were me would you understand why my heart races fearfully instead of calm beats or would I be better off being me escaping you, escaping me

● ● ●

Although it's good to laugh and have fun every once in a while, it's more important to make sure you pay attention to the kind of company you keep. Boyfriend, girlfriend or just a friend, when you begin to change and want more in life than what you're settling for and people aren't on the same page as you then you naturally commence to question the relationship or friendship. People begin to not make sense anymore and you question yourself if there's a good reason to continue communication with each other. Boyfriend for a few months or friend for several years, it doesn't matter because it's still the same kind of dead weight.

Ever notice when speaking to someone their attentiveness can vary in several ways? Either they aren't listening, looking at you like you've gone mad, their feelings get hurt by what you've said and more times than often they just really don't get it. You search for different ways to attempt gracefully escaping them according to their personality. Once before, I was in a relationship trapped because I became a prisoner of my own choices. Due to his inability to think logically I knew it was time to go, this wasn't the man I was supposed to be with. After finding my way through the maze it was a no brainer on how to get out of the artificial comfort I'd designed for myself. Getting out of a relationship appeared easier than ending a friendship that had years invested but I still managed to find a way out. Hopefully one day soon they'll finally get it and change for the better.

* * *

MENTOR ME

Hey little girl, where is your mother?
Can you tell me what she looks like?
Is she young, old
Short or tall
Tell me about her skin, can you see the color skin she's in?
What sort of words does she use?

Hey little girl, are you paying attention to me?
I need to speak to your mother
See I'm certain she doesn't know you're revealing yourself to
every other
Walking slumped over as though you've lost your spine
Someone has to help before you run out of time

Excuse me young lady, don't I know you from somewhere?
I know I've met you someplace before
When I was your age I stayed with my hands extended, heart
closed, ears full of wax and my mouth ran like faucet water
I swear you remind me so much of my daughter

Tell me sugar, who is your mother?
Need I ask permission to show attention to the reflection you
choose to ignore
Oh baby girl, you can be so more and then more
Don't you know you have to draw the line for yourself?
Use the forever marker so it'll never fade away
You'll see it even on those rainy days

Pardon me ma'am is everything okay?
The seasons have changed and you've been sitting here since
May
Submerged in sorrow drowning in tears
Oh baby it's been fifteen years

● ● ●

Engaged in ignorance, you have no idea
You need your mother by your side to help establish your future
She has wisdom thirsting to share with you

Do you know who your mother is?
Generation upon generation
She's paved the way for your generation
And so on and so forth
Press out the wrinkles above your brows
I'll help you build that confidence
A self-committing vow

Come here my child lets embrace for simplicity
Laugh at the presents of joy
Let me guide your hand as we paint a smile on your heart
Non void
Sealed with a kiss on the cheek
I've adopted you my sweet
And should someone ask you, who is your mother?
You tell them
She is me
She is you
The mother to be

* * *

God was my first choice. I asked Him to help me connect with someone who can lead me in the right direction. I needed someone who was married, had children, and success in their career. So I called a few people and no one answered. This wasn't a situation that I could just leave a voicemail, I needed help immediately. I made one last call to someone I didn't even have a number to, my auntie cousin. She's my cousin but I always looked at her like she was my aunt. She fit the category perfectly and more importantly she answered the phone, which had to have been the fastest I received a prayer answered because it was in matter of minutes. What awesome mercy and grace!

I poured my heart out to her. My struggles of being engaged with two children (same father and now my husband) reaching my epiphany and learning the word of God was the challenge. She told me everything the Holy Spirit put in her to say to me. The conversation got so deep that I pulled out my Bible while on the phone; as we went through a few appropriate scriptures, the answers, and the truth. She patiently listened to me through my sobbing. Though she has always been there for me if I need to talk to her, I looked at her like a mentor that day and every little girl needs a mentor.

I began to think about the women who've paved the way for my mentors. I have, we have, a responsibility to learn and continue learning from our mentors to teach the next generation and so on and so forth. So this poem was a cry out to my generation to wake up and begin to embrace our ancestors, our mothers, our strong women because time doesn't wait for anyone.

◦ ◦ ◦

SHEDDING NEW

Mr. Clean has one
As for the mechanical BIC
#1's and #2's
Even paper mate pens
All with one common denominator
The eraser
In a metaphorical sense I humor myself and get one on top of
me
Removing any form of energy that goes against my free will to
do me
To be me
I have to set you free from me

We naturally, unconsciously, and daily have the ability to shed
As I comb through my hair
Wash my silky smooth skin
When I release my toxins
While I cry and sweat
Even when I exhale
I release what is no need to me
Don't forget about a sneeze
Oh yes, God has blessed me
So why should I hold on to taunting old memories
Unhealthy friendships and that size ten dress
I feel fifteen pounds lighter already
Checking for a pulse to see if my heart still beats
Indeed, it does, absolutely I'm here
The engine to my car, it keeps me running
Without a doubt, I'm still here
Your conversation has gotten me to a place of nowhere
You haven't added value to my life
Nor to my mind since we've said hi
My name is...

* * *

And with a single careless stroke of the wrist
I've erased you just like that

• • •

There will be times in your life, if not already, when you'll have to make a decision to salvage it or trash it. Those who keep what isn't being put to use are defined as hoarders. Hoarders don't want to give anything away for the use of someone else nor do they want to trash it. They hold on to it for sentimental reasons. We do the same thing with people in our lives. Because we have history we hold on, because we had good times, because you make me laugh, because you helped me out and don't want to hurt your feeling we pick up the needle and thread and proceed to salvage what we don't want to get rid of. By not trashing it we hold on to the damaging, even nonproductive relationships and friendships.

Can you imagine how we would physically look if we didn't shed hair or skin and it continued to grow? What do you think we'd smell like if we never released any toxins? What if we only had the ability to inhale, what would that do to our bodies internally and externally? Sometimes friends are supposed to be seasonal so get over it and keep it moving.

＊ ＊ ＊

PORCELAIN MASK

Look at you
No
Now
When was the last time you took a good look at yourself?
Not the dressed up made up you
I'm talking about the bare you the real you
Can't stand to see the pain
You insist, let's put a smile on that face
Mixture of the foundation to get you started
Then the batting of the eyes shall lure them in
What color shall I choose today you say
Shimmer of the lips with a hint of pink and natural rosy red
cheeks
You've now transformed
Once human but now porcelain
You don't fool me
I can see right through you L'Oreal
Cause you still haven't fixed what's broken
Without the baby doll face you can't stand the sight
Won't tolerate the fight
They're all around you, north, south, east and west
They're all laughing at you as you try to look your best

Look at you
Don't walk away
You've glossed your smile, that's not why you're here
Lay your tweezers to rest, your brows are fine just clear your
face
I call you to search deep within the cornea straight to the soul
Confront those demons and forgive all yesterdays
Focus on today and tomorrow and not dwell on last years'
misconceptions
Take a good look and you'll see, you understand and so shall be
free

❋ ❋ ❋

Love within the mask
Experience life's joy you're guaranteed a blast
Say hello to the world bare and pure as a baby's bottom
Today I'll do the honors as I say
Good morning me I am new
I am you
Let's go do me

❀ ❀ ❀

Every notice how pretty a woman is when she's all dolled up? The hours of hair and make-up, tweezing and waxing? Some women don't even realize why they do it. Yeah sure it's to enhance your beauty, to be sexy or have to fun but whatever the reason you're covering up something on your face. Covering a black eye maybe? The kind you see or even a precedent black eye. Or maybe a black heart that pierces through the eye and tells all. To hide shame can be a subconscious common factor in wearing make-up. Sometimes we as women and men can't face ourselves when looking in the mirror because it is the truth. You are the only humane one who can really see straight through to the hurt and pain and pinpoint the problem.

It's tough trying to get the make-up all off. Make-up allows it to be an easier process but the hard part is being back in reality. It'll take work putting it on and work getting it off, whatever the case it may hurt both ways. So step out of your shell and love the skin you're in, find good in the bad and expose yourself. Don't be afraid to go bare every once in a while because a porcelain mask isn't necessary for every day. Periodically its' necessary to see yourself for who you are, past and present so that you may become capable to change your future. Remember, where ever you go, there you are.

❋ ❋ ❋

STRONG MOMMY

All by her lonesome
Just us and Mommy
She told us Daddy would be back

Dry your eyes sweetie, you'll see him again

With a splish and a splash
And sweet lullabies to follow all a glow

Goodnight, sweet dreams and I'll see you in the morning

All by her lonesome
Mommy cried to herself at the end of the night
Superpower strengths to continue on to the next
Day after day
Still no Daddy
Scratching and surviving
Creating good times to remember when while
He's not around
Bashing or no bashing you choose your mother
Because one of the two I guarantee she'll do
Drinking lemonade as often as possible to love the sweet and
sour taste
Loving them by sight because Mommy always know what to do
with them
Though she never said why lemons
Nor did she dread squeezing the yellow ovals
With a cheer in her voice and glee in her heart
She'd get excited as did we too
And when we sat on the porch without an ice cream
She'd break into that sock drawer and gathered what she could
Cause sooner or later the melody would hit the block
Mommy would beat us to it indeed she would

* * *

Out the window she stared at us and sometimes nothing
Inside I think that Mommy was crying

All by her lonesome
A particular time we broke her special vase
Horse playing and carrying on and throwing and whatnot
She scolded us good
Quietly she erased the mess
Regrouping in the bathroom, she must have had enough
To the door I listened
For some sort of sign that Mommy does cry
To say she'd had enough and that she needed Daddy, please
Resistance on the door, it could have been jammed

Mommy we're sorry I called

Quiet still and closer I listened again just once more
Nothing I heard, not even a sniffle
But half pass later she opened with a smile
Showering kisses, hugs, and tickles galore
Amazing strength I've inherited from my Mommy and those
before

* * *

STRONG MOMMY
Author's Elucidation

Inspired by single mothers everywhere, this poem was created in respect to them. My mother was a single mother of eight children and she didn't let us see when we were struggling. We were on welfare the majority of the time so we always had food in the house. She kept us in nice clothes (although not name brand most of the time) and a roof over our heads. Sometimes we were able to get name brand shoes if the owner was willing to make a deal because there were so many pairs of shoes to purchase and in most cases she got the deal because we lived in Chicago. Our house was from Section 8 but we had very nice furniture which was in every room. We went to the zoos, museums, circuses, ice shows, Six Flags (all the time) road trips and even attended a Nickelodeon show called Double Dare when it visited a city nearby. So we didn't really know we were poor until we got in high school.

She's not the only mother who conceals and do things to not show the struggle, there are many more. God's willing, I have a husband to help me. Some women don't have that luxury due to several reasons. Whenever I get overwhelmed as a mother all I have to do is tell my husband and the problem is solved. Having boys is even harder because a woman can't truly teach a boy to become a man. Certain things he wouldn't be able to relate to with his mother. I've learned how valuably important it is to have both parents in the household to help develop a balance with teaching and discipline. I couldn't imagine raising my children without my husband (male influence) but women do it every day without a choice and they don't give up. Some do their very best while others may tend to find something to drown out the sorrow. In any case, women who are single mothers have an inseparable bond and a remarkable amount of strength and courage. I salute you all, job well done.

* * *

A MOTHER'S GIFT

Can I be compelled to detail you about the brave choices you've
made thus far
With a typical nine-month glow just as you expected
Nevertheless, perfect or countable imperfections
Here I stand in the flesh in plain sight
Don't believe it blink twice
I am
Because of you
None mistaken for blame
I understand the real reason being
Embracing our history and loving with no shame
With flaws we could mention
Bad situations we could allow tension
I've mercerized my heart
And chose gracious words
I am peaceful
Because of you
Open to learn with each word that you speak
Please stay, willing to learn from me too
Inviting an indivisible link we continue to teach
I'm amazed at how much I do love you
To say to my siblings I've been there before I remember those
days, that week last year
Forgive your yesterday
Appreciate your today
As you still have time
Look on the bright side, see its right there
Every great moment has an uncompromising downside
Responsibility says to focus on the up and up
Brave you were to do everything you did
To be without and not let me go without
Right or wrong
Best or worst
A decision had to be made

* * *

Nonetheless
You helped create someone that no one can possibly duplicate
Me, she, him, and him
Her, her, this one and that
Giving us a chance was when you became brave

* * *

This piece has a very dear place in my heart because of its meaning. Having the breath of life is when you can appreciate a mother's gift. The inspiration behind this poem was a conversation my mother and I had about one of my siblings. As I recall, at that precise moment I heard her voice, she was furious and needed someone to side with her badly. She needed someone who had a big influence over my sibling so she called me to side with her. But I couldn't completely and honestly do that. My, oh my, was she hurt.

When I respectfully pointed out her flaws (with her permission) she was devastated because I said the same thing without even speaking to the feuding sibling. At that point my mother was convinced that she was a bad mother. I argued that she wasn't. As an adolescence I used to say the same thing but I didn't understand her place as a mother and what she stood for, my place nor did I know what good I had in her (you know the typical teenage drama). And I thought long and hard about what could possibly make her a bad mother but could think of nothing. I truly felt she was/is a great mother, flaws and all, if not then what's reason for me being who I am.

My mother loves me and has always loved me no matter what I did. With her help, I love me more now than ever and we have a great relationship. I was/am proud of my mommy and I couldn't have said that in my younger and teenage years. So when she attempted to confess she was a bad mother, she broke my heart. I didn't truly know what it meant to have my heart broken until then because my mother was the first person to ever break my heart. Although I wanted to, I couldn't cry because I had to be strong and show strength for her during a weak moment. Speaking for myself, my mother

● ● ●

was not and is not a bad mother, I, on the other hand was just immature and ignorant as with most teenagers. So this is a dedication to my mother to let her know that I mean what I say when I tell her, "You are not and have never been a bad mother and I've grown to understand and love a mother's gift".

Love You Mommy

* * *

REMEMBER ME...?

Toi Ragland

• • •

ABOUT THE AUTHOR

Born and raised on the south side of Chicago, Illinois, Toi Ragland was named La Toya Thompson to her mother Ms. Helen Thompson. Over the course of twelve years she became the second oldest of eight children birthed from Helen (having five sisters and two brothers). Toi attended James McCosh Elementary (now known as Emmitt Till), Vernon Johns Career Academy (formally known as Herman Raster Elementary), and Paul Laurence Dunbar Vocational High School. In high school she attended the Pom-Pom squad for four years. Very gifted, Toi learned how to become a wonderful hair stylist (thanks to the multiple siblings) and became a licensed cosmetologist graduating from Capri-Garfield Ridge Beauty College in 2002. The opportunity became available for Toi to relocate to Minnesota. For a few months there she stayed with her mother, step-father and six siblings. Determined to have her own space she got her CDL license and scored a job at Metro Transit (local transportation). There is when she met her husband during orientation day. Months later they moved in together. Before long, they became pregnant with a baby girl, five years later a baby boy and then marriage. Persistent to hold the physical copy of her years of dedication, hard work and joy of writing, Toi

* * *

made time in between being a wife, a mother and working part-time to complete and self-publish her first book of poetry. With many more books and projects to come stay tuned, stay connected and stay true.

* * *

Made in the USA
Columbia, SC
03 July 2019